SURPRISINGLY SCARY!

PUFFERFISH!

Dennis Rudenko

PowerKiDS press.

New York

Published in 2016 by The Rosen Publishing Group, Inc.
29 East 21st Street, New York, NY 10010

First Edition

Editor: Caitlin McAneney
Book Design: Katelyn Heinle

Photo Credits: Cover aastock/Shutterstock.com; back cover, pp. 3, 4, 6, 8, 10, 12, 14, 16, 18, 20, 22–24 (background) CAMPINCOOL/Shutterstock.com; pp. 4, 8 LauraD/Shutterstock.com; p. 5 Beth Swanson/Shutterstock.com; p. 7 (map pufferfish) Stubblefield Photography/Shutterstock.com; p. 7 (map inset) ekler/Shutterstock.com; p. 9 Bildagentur Zoonar GmbH/ Shutterstock.com; p. 10 (clam) amst/Shutterstock.com; p. 10 (tiger shark) Matt9122/Shutterstock.com; p. 11 Ian Scott/ Shutterstock.com; p. 13 Steven Hunt/Stone/Getty Images; p. 15 Vlad61/Shutterstock.com; p. 17 KPG_Payless/Shutterstock.com; p. 19 Michael Melford/The Image Bank/Getty Images; p. 21 Richard Whitcombe/Shutterstock.com; p. 22 Amir A/Shutterstock.com.

Library of Congress Cataloging-in-Publication Data

Rudenko, Dennis, author.
 Look out for the pufferfish! / Dennis Rudenko.
     pages cm. — (Surprisingly scary!)
 Includes bibliographical references and index.
 ISBN 978-1-4994-0881-2 (pbk.)
 ISBN 978-1-4994-0903-1 (6 pack)
 ISBN 978-1-4994-0950-5 (library binding)
 1. Puffers (Fish)—Juvenile literature. I. Title. II. Series: Surprisingly scary!
 QL638.T32R83 2016
 597.64—dc23
                                    2015012088

Manufactured in the United States of America

CPSIA Compliance Information: Batch #WS15PK: For Further Information contact Rosen Publishing, New York, New York at 1-800-237-9932

CONTENTS

DEADLY DEFENSES

Have you ever seen a pufferfish? You might not even recognize one if it were in its usual state. It looks like a regular fish, with small fins and a long snout. But when this fish is scared, it inflates like a balloon!

PUFFERFISH

Most people know the pufferfish because of this amazing **defense**. But did you know that these funny-looking fish are actually deadly? Pufferfish may look harmless, but they're one of the most poisonous creatures in the world.

Some pufferfish have spikes, which are called spines, that point out when the pufferfish inflates. The pufferfish's spiky body warns predators to stay far away!

SURPRISINGLY TRUE!

Pufferfish are also called puffers, blowfish, globefish, balloonfish, and toadfish.

MANY DIFFERENT SPECIES

Pufferfish live in many bodies of water around the world, especially in tropical, or warm, waters. While pufferfish usually like warm saltwater **habitats**, some kinds live in cooler salt water or freshwater.

The size, color, and poison of a pufferfish depend on its species, or kind. There are around 120 species of pufferfish. Some are tiny, while others are bigger. Some are one color, while others have markings of many colors. Some pufferfish use camouflage as a defense. Camouflage is the ability to blend into one's surroundings.

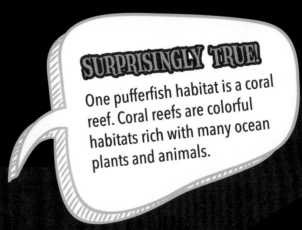

SURPRISINGLY TRUE!
One pufferfish habitat is a coral reef. Coral reefs are colorful habitats rich with many ocean plants and animals.

PUFFERFISH TERRITORY

ATLANTIC
OCEAN

PACIFIC
OCEAN

PACIFIC
OCEAN

INDIAN
OCEAN

A map pufferfish has dark markings all over its body that make it easy to blend in with its coral reef habitat.

BIZARRE BODIES

Many fish have scales, but not the pufferfish! Instead, pufferfish have spiky skin that feels rough to the touch. They have thin lower bodies that widen into a bigger head. Their fins are small and they don't swim very fast. Some pufferfish species are only 1 inch (2.5 cm) long, while others are nearly 3 feet (0.9 m) long!

A pufferfish's mouth sometimes looks like a beak. However, it's actually four teeth in the front of its mouth. Pufferfish teeth keep growing throughout their life, but they're worn down by crunchy meals.

TEETH

A pufferfish has fins on the top, back, bottom, and sides of its body. The side fins, or pectoral fins, help the pufferfish with direction and movement through the water.

PECTORAL FIN

SURPRISINGLY TRUE!

Pufferfish don't have a rib cage, and their stomach and skin can stretch far. That helps the pufferfish inflate.

PECTORAL FIN

WHAT'S FOR DINNER?

Pufferfish eat both sea animals and plant matter, which makes them omnivores. They like to eat algae, which are plantlike living things without roots. Algae grow on coral and rocks in reefs and also float in the water.

Pufferfish also eat small ocean creatures, especially those with shells. Eating shelled animals helps pufferfish keep their teeth from overgrowing. Larger pufferfish use their big teeth to crack open clams, shellfish, and mussels. Scientists think that a pufferfish's poison comes from bacteria in their meals.

CLAM

SURPRISINGLY TRUE!
Tiger sharks can eat pufferfish because the poison doesn't harm them.

Pufferfish are predators, but they're also **prey**. Pufferfish are hunted by sea snakes and larger fish, such as sharks.

INFLATABLE FISH

A pufferfish's ability to inflate is a defense that **developed** over millions of years. Animals develop defenses to keep them safe from other creatures in their habitat.

When a pufferfish sees a predator, it sucks in water through its mouth. It swallows the water to fill its stomach. The stomach stretches and makes the pufferfish much bigger. The predator may decide the pufferfish is too big to eat and leave it alone.

This pufferfish may look like it's holding its breath. However, it's actually breathing through its gills.

SURPRISINGLY TRUE!

When a pufferfish is out of water, it inflates by sucking in air.

THE POISONOUS PUFFER

Venomous creatures **inject** their poison into another creature. Poisonous creatures, such as the pufferfish, hold their poison in their body. That's bad news for animals or people who touch them or take a bite.

The pufferfish's poison is called tetrodotoxin. The pufferfish's spiky skin holds this poison. Certain body parts are also filled with it, so animals that eat pufferfish often die. Tetrodotoxin causes **paralysis** in the unlucky animal or person. There is no **antidote** to a pufferfish's poison.

The tetrodotoxin in one pufferfish is enough to kill 30 people.

SURPRISINGLY TRUE!

Not all pufferfish are poisonous, but some are more poisonous than others.

A DEADLY DISH

If we *know* pufferfish are deadly, why would someone eat one? Surprisingly enough, many people eat pufferfish as a special dish. This dish, called fugu, is popular in Japan.

Fugu is prepared by chefs who are specially trained in the art of cutting a pufferfish. If the fish is cut the right way, it makes for a yummy treat. If it's cut the wrong way, people can die. Fugu chefs train for about three years to get a **license** to prepare pufferfish.

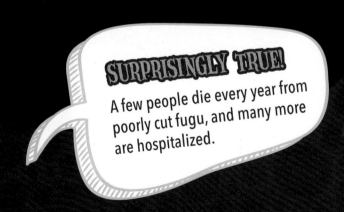

SURPRISINGLY TRUE!

A few people die every year from poorly cut fugu, and many more are hospitalized.

A plate of fugu can cost up to $200!

PUFFERFISH AND PEOPLE

What happens when a person is poisoned by a pufferfish? Within minutes, the person might feel an itching or tickling feeling in their mouth and lips. They might get a headache or feel like throwing up. Then, the person may pass out, become paralyzed, or even die. It's important to get help right away.

Most of the pufferfish's poison is held inside its body. However, sometimes the poison can be let out of its skin. Fishermen wear thick gloves when handling pufferfish to keep themselves safe.

Touching a pufferfish might not poison you, but you might get a nasty bite! A pufferfish's hard teeth can cause a lot of damage.

PROTECTING THE PUFFERFISH

Pufferfish live in many kinds of habitats all over the world. They've developed defenses to keep them safe from other creatures. Still, some pufferfish populations are at risk.

While many species of pufferfish are doing well, some populations are considered **threatened**. Habitat loss is a major reason for population decline. Also, the pufferfish used to make fugu are sometimes overfished. Pufferfish might be risky to touch or eat, but we have a duty to keep them around for a long time.

SURPRISINGLY TRUE!

The Malabar, or dwarf, pufferfish is considered threatened because people have destroyed and changed its habitat and because many are taken for the pet trade.

This is a dead coral reef. Human activities harm the coral reefs where many pufferfish make their home.

DON'T MESS WITH A PUFFERFISH!

Pufferfish are defensive fish you don't want to mess with! Their strong, hard teeth can give a nasty bite. Their spiky skin and some of their **organs** are poisonous. These defenses keep pufferfish safe from the many other creatures that live in their underwater habitats.

Some people keep pufferfish as pets, and they have to learn how to properly care for them so both the fish and owner are safe. When it comes to pufferfish, it's best not to touch or take a bite!

GLOSSARY

aggressive: Showing a readiness to attack.

antidote: Something that stops the harmful effects of poison.

defense: A way of guarding against an enemy.

develop: Growing and changing over time.

habitat: The natural home for plants, animals, and other living things.

inflate: To grow bigger as air or water is forced into something.

inject: To force something into the body.

license: An official paper that gives someone permission to do something.

organ: A body part that does a certain task.

paralysis: The state of being unable to move.

prey: An animal hunted by other animals for food.

snout: An animal's nose and mouth.

threatened: Likely to be harmed.

INDEX

WEBSITES

Due to the changing nature of Internet links, PowerKids Press has developed an online list of websites related to the subject of this book. This site is updated regularly. Please use this link to access the list: www.powerkidslinks.com/surp/puff